What's So Hot About the sun?

And Other Questions about...
Outer Space

Roger
Howerton

Master
Books

When the United States sent the first mission (Apollo 11) to the moon in 1969, several pieces of equipment were sent along for experiments. One piece of equipment was a small reflector that was left on the moon for measuring the distance from the earth to the moon. This reflector is very small, only 46 cm (18 in) square. Scientists can now send laser beams to the reflector from earth, and precisely measure the time it takes for the beam to reflect back to earth. Knowing that the laser beams travel at the speed of light (299,792.458 km/sec or 186,282mi/sec), scientists are able to calculate the precise distance from the earth to the moon.

The reflector measurements have indicated that the earth and moon are moving apart at a rate of about 3.82 cm (about 1.5 in) per year.

Take Nothing but Pictures, Leave Nothing but Footprints:
Because the moon has no atmosphere, it has no wind or weather, so everything on its surface stays the same. The footprints and American flag left by the astronauts in 1969 are still there.

Ask Max!

Way to Grow!

When astronauts returned from an eighty-four-day space mission in 1974, they had grown two inches taller! Here's why: In a weightless environment, the spinal disks in the back absorb more fluid and expand, causing the person to become taller. Within a few days of reaching earth, however, the astronauts shrank back to their normal heights.

Q. Where do moon people go after they get married?

A. On their honeyearth!

Q. Did you hear about the new restaurant on the moon?

A. Yeah, great food, but no atmosphere.

Beware of the Full Moooooon:

The words "lunacy" and "lunatic" come from the Latin word luna, meaning "moon." It was once believed that sleeping in moonlight would cause madness. This may also be where the phrase, "moonlight madness" comes from.

How Did the Ancient Greeks Know That the Earth Is Round?

Simple. Aristotle, a noted scientist and philosopher, pointed out that a lunar eclipse was caused when the earth moved between the sun and the moon, casting its shadow on the moon. In a partial eclipse of the moon, the shadow of the earth is round, and therefore, the earth is round.

The Greeks also noticed the curvature of the earth because as ships would sail out of sight, the last part of the ship that was visible was the sail. A disappearing vessel seemed to be going over a hill.

Lunar Eclipse

Ask Max!

Q. Where did Columbus first land in America?

A. On his feet!

Genoa 'Bout Columbus, Right?

When Columbus sought financing for his voyage from the crowned heads of Europe, all of the courts (except Spain) rejected him — but not because they thought the earth was flat. They rejected him because they believed Asia was too far to be reached by ship — and they were right. Columbus had greatly misjudged the circumference of the earth. He thought the earth was much smaller than it is and he was not prepared for the very long voyage it would have taken to reach Asia. If Columbus had not accidentally discovered the Americas, he and his crew would have perished in the vast ocean before reaching the East.

Flat as a Pancake:

Many leaders in the church of the fourth through the eighth centuries held that the ancient scientific theories of a round earth were false. One church leader in Alexandria, Egypt could not figure out how anyone or anything could be on the underside of the earth. He envisioned people upside down, rain falling upward, and he completely denounced the anti-biblical idea of the heavens being lower than the earth.

Thankfully, the flat-earth theory persisted only through the Dark Ages. By the ninth century — long before the voyages of Columbus — the ancient Greek and Roman teachings of a round earth became popular once more in Europe, and thoughts of a round earth were again believable.

What Are Other Planets Made Of?

We actually know very little about what the other planets are made of. Mercury is thought to be mostly iron. Venus has had a lot of volcanic activity, and has sand dunes, mountains and valleys. Mars is known as the "Red Planet," because its surface has a lot of iron oxide (better known as rust). The atmosphere of Mars is mostly carbon dioxide. Breathing it would be like breathing car exhaust. Jupiter, Saturn, Uranus and Neptune are mostly gases — they may or may not have solid surfaces. Pluto, unlike the huge "gas-ball" planets has hardly any atmosphere at all. Scientists think it may have a rocky core surrounded by ice.

How to Remember the Order of the Planets:

My Very Earnest Mother Just Sent Us New Pencils.

M	V	E	M	J	S	U	N	P
E	E	A	A	U	A	R	E	L
R	N	R	R	P	T	A	P	U
C	U	T	S	I	U	N	T	T
U	S	H		T	R	U	U	O
R				E	N	S	N	
Y				R			E	

Ask Max!

Old Reliable:

Halley's Comet is probably the most well-known comet. (Correct pronunciation: "Halley" rhymes with "valley.") It returns every 76 years and will appear in the sky again in the year 2061. Interesting to note: Halley's Comet appeared the year Mark Twain was born and reappeared the year he died.

All Things Work Together:

Why did God even make other planets? In the Book of Genesis, God declared that He had made them for signs, seasons, days and years, and to give light. Although the planets are separated by thousands of miles, they move in perfect harmony, stabilizing the solar system.

Which Came First?

Pluto was named by the eleven-year-old daughter of an Oxford astronomy professor. She named it after a pagan god. The Disney character, Pluto, made his debut the same year that the planet was discovered (1930) and was named after the planet.

Jeweler's Delight:

Saturn has more than 100,000 rings.

What Are Some Fun Facts about the Solar System?

The Whopper:

Jupiter, the largest planet, is more than 1,000 times larger than Earth.

Hey, Shrimp!

Pluto, the smallest planet, is 143 times smaller than Earth.

Hot Spot:

The hottest planet is Venus. Better take your sunscreen. Daytime highs can exceed 900° F. This is cool in comparison to the surface of the sun, which is about 10,000° F.

Baby, It's Cold Outside:

The coldest planet is the one farthest from the sun — Pluto. With an average temperature of -370° F, Pluto is no trip to Disney World. If the Earth were as cold as Pluto, nearly all the gases in our atmosphere would be frozen solid.

Jupiter

Pluto

This Is the Storm that Never Ends:

The "Great Red Spot" on Jupiter is a massive cyclone large enough to swallow several Earths and has been raging at least since Galileo first saw it in the 1600s. (above)

Older than Methuselah:

The oldest planet is Earth, created "in the beginning," while the other planets were created on the fourth day of Creation. The entire solar system is only six or seven thousand years old, give or take a day.

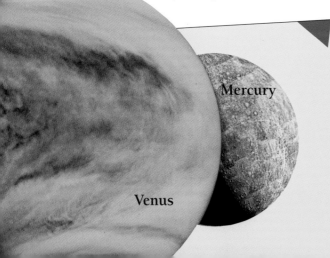

Mercury

Venus

I Thought that Day Would Never End:

Weekends would be great on Mercury, where the day is 176 Earth days long. Ironically, a day on Mercury lasts twice as long as its year, which, at 88 days is the shortest year in the solar system.

Tons of Fun:

Gravity on Jupiter is two-and-a-half times that of the Earth. To find out how much you would weigh on Jupiter, multiply your weight by 2.5. For example if you weight 120 lbs. on Earth, you would weigh 300 lbs. on Jupiter.

East Is East and West Is West, but This is Ridiculous!

Venus, Uranus, and Pluto spin "backward" when compared to the rotation of the other six planets. This means that the sun rises in the west and sets in the east on these three planets. Talk about confusing!

Featherweight:

Gravity on the moon is one-sixth of what it is on Earth. To find out how much you would weigh on the moon, divide your weight by six. For example, if you weigh 120 lbs. on Earth, you would only weigh 20 lbs. on the moon.

Talk About Moon Glow!

Saturn and Uranus are tied for having the most number of moons. On these planets, you could take a walk in the evening and watch the moons come up — all 18 of them! The total number of known moons in the solar system is 63.

Uranus

But It's Not Snow-Covered:

Olympus Mons, the tallest mountain in the solar system is on Mars. It is twice as high as Mt. Everest and covers an area half as large as Texas. Of course, Texans would claim "that ain't so big. . . ."

Grander Canyon:

The deepest canyon in the solar sysem is Valles Marineris, also on Mars. It is twice as deep and ten times as wide as the Grand Canyon. Watch that first step — it's a lulu! (below)

Saturn

Every object in the universe is constantly moving, and sometimes objects will move in front of other objects. An eclipse happens when one celestial body (moon, earth, planet) moves in front of another celestial body. (During the next full moon, hold a dime out from your eyes to block the moon. This will give you a good idea of an eclipse.) We are most familiar with solar (sun) and lunar (moon) eclipses.

A solar eclipse occurs when the moon comes between the earth and the sun, and makes a shadow on the earth. A lunar eclipse occurs when the earth is between the sun and the moon, casting a shadow on the moon. During a lunar eclipse, the moon will shine a dull red, and will look like a sunset because of the refraction (bending of light) of sunlight around the earth. Note: A lunar eclipse is not what you see when you see the phases (first quarter, half moon, full moon, etc.) of the moon.

Sun

Lunar Eclipse

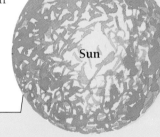

Sun

Solar Eclipse

Moon

Solar Eclipse

Mark Your Calendar!

The next total eclipse that will be visible from the United States will be on August 21, 2017 in a narrow path all the way from Oregon to South Carolina.

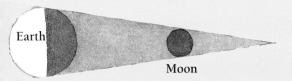

Earth

Moon

Lunar Eclipse

Who Turned Out the Lights?

During the 20th century, 375 eclipses took place: 228 solar and 147 lunar.

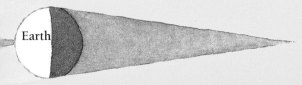

Earth

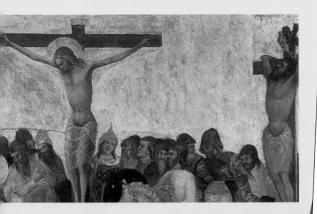

Was It a Miracle?

When Christ was crucified for all of our sins, the Bible tells us that there was darkness "from the sixth hour. . . unto the ninth hour" (Matt. 27:45). Since the daytime hours of that time were counted beginning at 6 a.m., this would be darkness from noon (the "sixth hour") until 3:00. Was this an eclipse? If we review some historical facts, we will learn that this darkness could not have been an eclipse.

First of all, we know that the crucifixion of Christ happened at the Jewish feast of Passover (John 13:1). Second, the Jewish calendar was manipulated each year so that Passover would occur at the full moon. Third, during the phase of the full moon, the moon is on the opposite side of the earth from the sun. Since a solar eclipse is caused when the moon passes between the earth and the sun, an eclipse during a full moon is impossible. Therefore, the darkness at the crucifixion was not a coincidental eclipse, but a supernatural miracle of God.

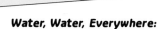

The moon cannot support life of any kind. Although the earth and moon receive approximately the same amount of sunlight, the moon cannot block the extreme heat during the day nor retain any heat during the night because it has no water or atmosphere. Temperatures on the surface of the moon are extreme, ranging from a maximum of 261° F (127° C) at lunar noon to a minimum of -279° F (-173° C) just before lunar dawn. No one could survive these harsh conditions without adequate protection.

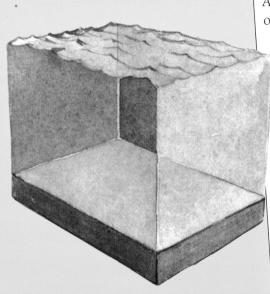

Water, Water, Everywhere:

All life requires liquid water for survival. There is no liquid water on the moon. Of course, drinking water could be shuttled to the moon at a great expense, but earth's water does so much more than just give us something to drink.

The salt water of the oceans may seem useless to us since we can't drink it. We probably think there is too much ocean water, but every drop is needed. Water retains the sun's heat better than the land does. Without all of our oceans, the earth would gradually become colder and colder. The huge surface of the oceans also provides the evaporated water that eventually falls as fresh rain over the land, giving water to all animals and vegetation there.

In fact, so much of the earth is water that if all of the solid material were completely smooth, the earth would be covered by a solid ocean of water over a mile and a half deep!

Ask Max!

Where in the World Is All of the Water?

Less than one percent of the earth's water is all that is available at any one time for the use of her six billion inhabitants! That available water is in the air, streams, lakes, and underground:

Percent	Location
97.4	oceans
2.0	ice, glaciers
0.58	underground
0.011	streams
0.009	atmosphere
100.00%	

Rightful Air:

The earth's atmosphere provides a necessary "blanket" around the earth. It gives us the air that we breathe. Air for breathing could be shipped to the moon, but the moon could not provide the air itself. The atmosphere shelters us from the harmful rays of the sun. It helps retain the heat needed for life on earth.

I Wonder What the In-flight Movie Was?

A California man paid a reported 20 million dollars to the Russian space program to be the first ordinary citizen in orbit. His was a round-trip, eight-day visit to the International Space Station ending on May 6, 2001.

Why Do Stars Twinkle?

The answer has to do with distance. Planets are in our own solar system, and although they are millions of miles from the earth, they are still much closer than the stars, which are trillions of miles from the earth. It takes years for the light from a star to reach the earth, so, by the time the light reaches the earth, it is a tiny, weak ray of light that is easily affected by the ripples in our atmosphere. The light from planets, although it is only a reflection of the sun's light, is still much stronger than the distant stars' light, and is not affected by variations in the earth's atmosphere. Therefore, stars twinkle, but planets don't.

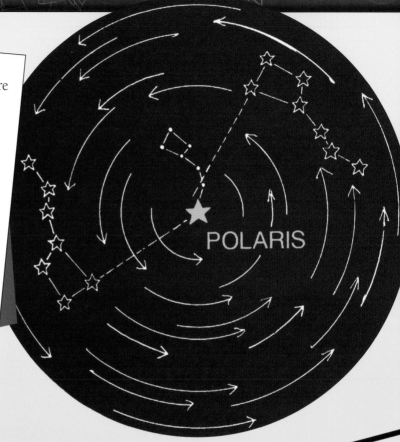

POLARIS

93,000,000 miles
8 minutes

Faster Than You Can Say Jack Robinson:

It only takes 8 minutes for the light from the sun to travel the 93 million miles to earth!

Ask Max!

Star Light, Star Bright:

The closest star to our solar system is Proxima Centauri, four and a half light years away. This means that it takes four and a half years for light from Proxima Centauri to reach our solar system.

atie: I'm going to make a trip to the moon!

aleb: That's nothing new. Others have been there!

atie: Well, maybe I'll go to Mars.

aleb: Nah, that's not exciting.

atie: Okay, then, where are you going to go?

Kaleb: I'm going to go to the sun!

Katie: You can't go to the sun; you'll burn up!

Kaleb: No I won't. I'm planning to go at night!

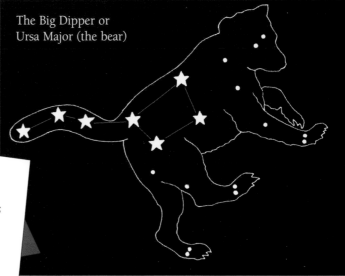

The Big Dipper or Ursa Major (the bear)

How Far Is a Light Year?

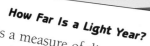

A light year is a measure of distance, not time. It is the distance that light can travel in a year. Since light travels at about 186,000 miles per second, and there are 31,536,000 seconds in a year, a light year would be around six trillion miles!

Why Do We Always See the Same Side of the Moon?

If you look at the moon on different occasions, you will sooner or later begin to notice that it always looks the same. This is because we are seeing the same side all of the time. Why don't we ever see the other side (what is known as the "dark side") of the moon? It is because the period of time the moon takes to rotate one time is exactly the same period of time the moon takes to revolve around the earth one time: exactly 27 days, 7 hours, and 43.2 minutes. The rotation of the moon keeps the same side facing the earth at all times.

The moon as seen from space

Distance from the Earth to the Moon?

239,000 miles

Earth

Courtney: Have you heard that they have found life on other planets?

Kyle: Yeah, they found fleas on Pluto!

Peek-A-Boo:

No man had ever seen the "dark side" of the mo until 1959 when it was photographed by the Soviet space vehicle Lunik III.

Ask Max!

Experiment:

You'll need:

- Ping pong ball, tennis ball, or racquetball
- Something to make an axis in the ball with adult help
- Magic marker – black
- Dinner plate

Ask an adult for help!!

1. Take an old ping-pong ball, tennis ball, or racquetball to represent the moon.

2. Color one half (hemisphere) of it black to represent the dark side.

3. Let Mom or Dad or another adult make an axis through the center of the ball using a long, pointed object.

4. Next, lay a circular dinner plate on a table to represent the earth.

5. Position the ball on the table a couple of inches from the plate with the dark side facing away from the plate.

6. Now, make a revolution around the plate with the ball, keeping the dark side always facing away.

Do you see that in order to keep the dark side facing away, you must rotate the ball on its axis? By the time you return to the starting point of the revolution, you have rotated the ball exactly one time. If you do not rotate the ball, all sides of it will face the plate at some point in the revolution. In much the same way, the moon rotates as it revolves around the earth, always keeping the same side toward the earth.

Moon

Why Does the Moon Appear Larger near the Horizon?

This is one of God's great optical illusions. Of course the moon is no larger when it is rising than when it is high in the sky. It only appears larger because we tend to judge the size of anything by comparing it to something else that is nearby. In this case, we are probably comparing the rising moon to a tree or building and the moon really seems huge.

The same effects also happen with sunrises and sunsets. God has given us beautiful starts and finishes to our day with these beautiful phenomena.

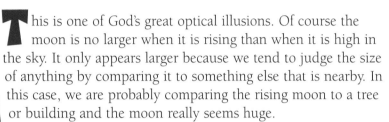

Full Moon   Quart

Shine On, Harvest Moon:
The full moon occurring nearest the autumnal equinox (September 21 or 22) is called Harvest Moon. The next full moon is called Hunter's Moon.

Ask Max!

Experiment:

You'll need:

• tube from the center of a roll of paper towels

To prove that the moon does not shrink as it rises, take an ordinary tube from the center of a roll of paper towels. As the full moon is rising near the horizon, look at it through the tube. Later, when the moon gets high into the sky, look at it again through the tube. You should observe that it occupies the same amount of space inside of the tube as it did when you looked at it near the horizon.

Moon Rock

Q. Why is a moon rock better for you than an earth rock?

A. Because it's a little meatier (meteor).

Optical Illusion:

Look at the two circles in the center of each group. Which is larger?

Actually, they are the same size. The one on the left appears larger because of its placement in the center of the smaller circles. Our eyes tend to compare things to whatever they are near, just as we compare the rising moon to other things nearby.

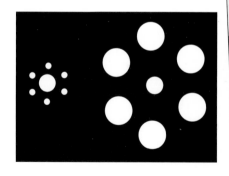

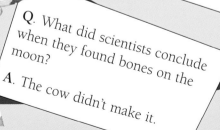

Q. What did scientists conclude when they found bones on the moon?

A. The cow didn't make it.

Why Is the Sky Blue?

S unlight is composed of all colors: red, orange, yellow, green, blue, violet, and every possibility in between. Every color has a "wavelength," which makes it visible to our eyes. Red has the longest, while blue and violet — at the other end of the spectrum (the band of colors) — have the shortest. As all of these colors pass through space, they move in a straight line. But when they enter the atmosphere, the colors hit tiny gas molecules. The colors with longer wavelengths are not affected, and pass straight through, but the shorter wavelengths of blue and violet bounce off of the gas molecules, and "scatter" in the sky. Even though the violet wavelengths scatter more than the blue because they are shorter, the sun gives off much more blue light than violet, and so the sky is blue.

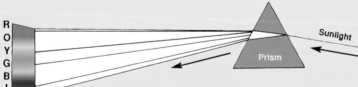

R
O
Y
G
B
I
V

Sunlight

Prism

Make That Supersize:

The sun is the largest body in the solar system. It is nearly 1,000,000 miles across and could contain more than 1,000,000 Earth-sized planets.

Why Is the Sky Red at Sunset?

When we look at a sunrise or sunset, we are viewing it through the lowest layer of atmosphere, which is "thicker" because it contains not only those gas molecules mentioned earlier, but also a lot of moisture, dust, and other impurities. The sunlight is entering the atmosphere at an angle, and must pass through more of this thick air than it does when it is high in the sky. The impurities of this thicker atmosphere scatter even more of the colors including the yellow and orange, leaving only the longest wavelengths of red to reach our eyes, giving the sun its deep red color. God, the Master Artist, established all of the laws of science, including those that give us golden sunrises and fiery sunsets.

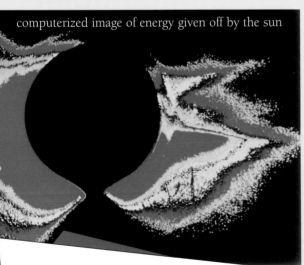

computerized image of energy given off by the sun

Heavenly Sunlight:

The sun gives the earth six million times more light than all the other stars combined.

Will the Sun Ever Become a Shooting Star?

Have you ever seen a shooting star? It looks like a bright star has suddenly jumped from its place and darted across the sky. Our sun is a star, so what keeps it from springing out of its position and shooting across the galaxy at any moment?

Actually, shooting stars are not stars at all, but are meteors. Probably when you think of meteors, you think of huge, monstrous rocks floating around in space. Most meteors are not huge rocks, but are actually the size of pebbles or sand. Hundreds of these meteors enter the earth's atmosphere each day. When they enter our atmosphere, they become extremely hot from the friction and burn brightly. They usually burn up in a few seconds, never reaching the ground. These fine, glowing granules are what we call shooting stars.

Photo of actual meteorite

Did God Make a Mistake?

In Genesis 22:17, God promised Abraham that his descendants would be as numerous as the stars of the heaven and the sand upon the seashore. For centuries, this verse did not make sense. At the most, there were only 6,000 visible stars, but there were billions of grains of sand on the seashore. Had God made a mistake?

The problem began to be resolved when Galileo became the first person to look at the stars through a telescope in the 1600s. He saw many, many more stars through a telescope than could be seen with the unaided eye. As telescopes have become more and more powerful in the centuries since Galileo, astronomers have found that there are billions and billions of stars. Scientists tell people that a good way to imagine the billions of stars is simply to think of the grains of sand on the seashores.

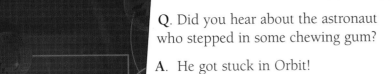

Q. Did you hear about the astronaut who stepped in some chewing gum?

A. He got stuck in Orbit!

James W. Young - 1966

Twinkle, Twinkle:

On a clear night, you can see about 2,000 stars. Astronomers, with high-powered telescopes, can see billions of stars.

Solar flares on the sun

Super Bowl Super Hole:

Meteor Crater, near Winslow, Arizona, is evidence of one of the largest meteors ever to hit the earth. It is around 600 feet deep and 1 mile across. Twenty football games could be played simultaneously on its floor while two million spectators could watch from the slopes of the crater.

First printing: February 2002

ISBN: 0-89051-364-3
Library of Congress Number: 2001098882

Printed in the United States of America

Please visit our website for other great titles:
www.masterbooks.net

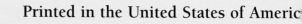